Jaguars

by Claire Archer

www.abdopublishing.com

Published by Abdo Kids, a division of ABDO, P.O. Box 398166, Minneapolis, Minnesota 55439.

Copyright © 2015 by Abdo Consulting Group, Inc. International copyrights reserved in all countries. No part of this book may be reproduced in any form without written permission from the publisher.

Printed in the United States of America, North Mankato, Minnesota.

052014

092014

 THIS BOOK CONTAINS RECYCLED MATERIALS

Photo Credits: iStock, Shutterstock, Thinkstock

Production Contributors: Teddy Borth, Jennie Forsberg, Grace Hansen

Design Contributors: Candice Keimig, Laura Rask, Dorothy Toth

Library of Congress Control Number: 2013952100

Cataloging-in-Publication Data

Archer, Claire.

 Jaguars / Claire Archer.

   p. cm. -- (Big cats)

ISBN 978-1-62970-002-1 (lib. bdg.)

Includes bibliographical references and index.

1. Jaguars--Juvenile literature.   I. Title.

599.755--dc23

                    2013952100

Table of Contents

Jaguars 4

Hunting 14

Food 16

Baby Jaguars 18

More Facts 22

Glossary 23

Index 24

Abdo Kids Code 24

Jaguars

Jaguars live in South and Central America and Mexico. They live in many different **habitats**.

Jaguars usually live in

areas with lots of plants.

You will almost always

find them living near water.

Jaguars usually have tan or orange fur. They have black spots called rosettes.

9

Jaguars are sometimes completely black. Their spots are hard to see.

Jaguars are big cats.

Only big cats can roar.

13

Hunting

Jaguars usually hunt on the ground. They sometimes hide in trees.

15

Food

Jaguars are meat-eaters.

They eat deer, turtles,

fish, and much more.

17

Baby Jaguars

Jaguars have one to four babies at a time.

They often have **twins**.

Baby jaguars are called cubs.

Cubs learn everything from

their mothers.

21

More Facts

- Jaguars are closely related to leopards.
  It can be very hard to tell them apart.

- A jaguar's fur helps it to hide in its **habitat**.
  This is called camouflage.

- A jaguar's bite is two times as strong as a lion's
  bite. Its jaw can bite through a turtle's shell.

Glossary

cub – a young animal.

habitat – a place where a living thing is naturally found.

rosette – a marking that resembles a rose.

twins – two animals born at the same time from one mother.

Index

babies 18, 20

Central America 4

fur 8, 10

habitat 4, 6

hunting 14

markings 8, 10

Mexico 4

prey 16

size 12

South America 4

abdokids.com

Use this code to log on to abdokids.com and access crafts, games, videos and more!

Abdo Kids Code:
BJK0021